God's Words About You

Poems and compilation by PJ Lolly

WestBow Press books may be ordered through booksellers or by contacting:

WestBow Press
A Division of Thomas Nelson & Zondervan
1663 Liberty Drive
Bloomington, IN 47403
www.westbowpress.com
844-714-3454

ISBN: 978-1-6642-6509-7 (sc)
ISBN: 978-1-6642-6510-3 (e)

Library of Congress Control Number: 2022907843

Print information available on the last page.

WestBow Press rev. date: 5/5/2022

WestBow
PRESS®
A DIVISION OF THOMAS NELSON
& ZONDERVAN

Preface

When Jesus comes to live in your heart, He brings all of Father God's promises to you. This little book shares some of those promises and shows you how to make them your own so you can learn that God loves, values, guides, celebrates, and protects you. I hope you enjoy these poems and grow to know the goodness of God who sent His Son, Jesus, to take your punishment and make you His child.

If you have never asked Jesus to live in your heart and would like to, you can pray the following prayer.

Father God, thank You for loving me so much that You sent Jesus to pay the price of my disobedience. Jesus, thank You for dying on the cross for me and making all of God's promises true for me. I want You to live in my heart. Help me to trust You, follow You, and believe God's promises. Thank You for coming into my heart to give me a good life now and eternal life with You forever. Amen.

Now, start reading this book and begin learning about all the wonderful things God says about you.

Born, adopted, married, and bought—
I'm loved by God, and by Him I'm sought.
As I love God with all my heart,
Entering His family, God will impart.

I am born, adopted, married, and bought into the family of God.

BORN – John 3:5-7 "...Truly, truly, I say to you, unless one is born of water and the Spirit, he cannot enter the kingdom of God...You must be born again. English Standard Version

ADOPTED –Galatians 4:5 "God sent him (Jesus) to buy freedom for us who were slaves to the law, so that he could adopt us as his very own children." New Living Translation

MARRIED – Revelation 19:7 "Let us be glad and rejoice, and give honor to him: for the marriage of the Lamb is come, and his wife hath made herself ready." King James Version

BOUGHT – I Corinthians 6:20 "For ye are bought with a price: therefore glorify God in your body, and in your spirit, which are God's." New King James Version

Many good things God gives His kids.
His promise is true as I follow God's bids.
Because I believe that God sent His Son,
Eternal life I have now won.

Because I believe that God sent His son to die for me, I have eternal life.

John 3:16 "For God so loved the world that he gave his one and only Son, that whoever believes in him shall not perish but have eternal life." New International Version

Fearfully, wonderfully I'm surely made.
God cheerfully, lovingly designed and arrayed.
I am so perfect just as God planned.
I'm a real kid sketched out by God's hand.

I am fearfully and wonderfully made.

Psalm 139:14 "I praise you for I am fearfully and wonderfully made. Marvelous are Your works, and I know this very well." Berean Study Bible

The Lord is my shepherd, so I surely know
All that I need, God freely bestows.
All that I need for life in this world
Was given by Jesus when His grace was unfurled.

Because the Lord is my shepherd, I have everything I need.
God has given me everything I need for life and godliness.

Psalm 23:1 "The Lord is my shepherd; I have all that I need." New International Version

II Peter 1:3 "His divine power has given us everything required for life and godliness through the knowledge of him who called us by his own glory and goodness." Christian Standard Bible

On the cross Jesus died for all of my sins.
Forgiveness is mine and new life begins.
God's blessings are mine; I love Him so.
In the city, the country, wherever I go.

God blesses me in the city, the country, going out, and coming in.

Deuteronomy 28:3, 6 "Blessed shall you be in the city, and blessed shall you be in the country...Blessed shall you be when you come in, and blessed shall you be when you go out." New King James Version

Angels protect me wherever I go.
I follow God's voice, for He loves me so.
Fear is not mine; He's made me whole.
I'm filled with love, strength, and much self-control.

I am protected by angels.
I follow the good Shepherd for I know His voice.
God has not given me a spirit of fear; but of power, love, and self-control.

Psalm 91:11 "For He will give His angels orders concerning you, to protect you in all your ways." Holman Christian Standard Bible

John 10:3-4 "The gatekeeper opens the gate for him, and the sheep listen to his voice. He calls his own sheep by name and leads them out. When he has brought out all his own, he goes on ahead of them, and his sheep follow him because they know his voice." New International Version

II Timothy 1:7 "God did not give us a spirit that makes us afraid but a spirit of power and love and self-control." New Century Version

Troubles will come, but God's promise is clear.
He will protect because I am held dear.
With nothing to fear, I can rest and receive
God's bountiful blessings overtaking my need.

Troubles may come to me, but the Lord will deliver me from them all.
God is chasing me down and overtaking me with His blessings.

Psalm 34:19 "The Lord's people may suffer a lot, but he will always bring them safely through." Contemporary English Version

Deuteronomy 28:6 "Wherever you go and whatever you do, you will be blessed." New Living Translation

Because I delight in the law of my Lord,
I grow and I flourish like a tree by the shore.
God's plan for me is to prosper and grow.
I'll follow His lead and watch His plan flow.

Because my delight is in the law of the Lord, I am
like a tree planted by rivers of water.
God's plan for me is to prosper me and give me hope and a future.

Psalm 1:1-3 "Oh, the joys of those who do not follow the advice of the wicked, or stand around with sinners, or join in with mockers. But they delight in the law of the Lord, meditating on it day and night. They are like trees planted along the riverbank, bearing fruit each season. Their leaves never wither, and they prosper in all they do." New Living Translation

Jeremiah 29:11 "'For I know the plans I have for you,' declares the Lord, 'plans to prosper you and not to harm you, plans to give you hope and a future.'" New International Version

Laughter and pleasure are God's gifts to me.
He's a good Father, and love is His key.
It's always His goodness leading me to repent,
And never unkindness does He present.

Laughter and pleasure are gifts to me from God.
God's kindness leads me to repentance.

Ecclesiastes 5:18-20 "Even so, I have noticed one thing, at least, that is good. It is good for people to eat, drink, and enjoy their work under the sun during the short life God has given them, and to accept their lot in life. And it is a good thing to receive wealth from God and the good health to enjoy it. To enjoy your work and accept your lot in life—this is indeed a gift from God. God keeps such people so busy enjoying life that they take no time to brood over the past." New Living Translation

Romans 2:4 "...God's kindness is intended to lead you to repentance." Christian Standard Bible

Jesus came here my debt to redeem.
Resurrected, He lives, and love is His theme.
Setting me free was so very high priced,
But I am victorious through my Lord, Jesus Christ.

I am victorious through Jesus Christ.

I Corinthians 15:57 "But thanks be to God! He gives us the victory through our Lord Jesus Christ." New International Version

Printed in the United States
by Baker & Taylor Publisher Services